Snow Friends

by Deb Strain

Landauer Books

Snow Friends
by Deb Strain

Copyright© 2002 by Landauer Corporation
Designs and Projects Copyright© 2002 by Deb Strain, Licensed by Mosaic

This book was designed, produced, and published by Landauer Books
A division of Landauer Corporation
12251 Maffitt Road, Cumming, Iowa 50061

President/Publisher: Jeramy Lanigan Landauer
Executive Vice President Sales & Marketing: James L. Knapp
Executive Vice President Editorial: Becky Johnston
Creative Director: Laurel Albright
Project Editor: M. Peg Smith
Project Designer: Margaret Sindelar
Technical Writer: Sylvia Miller
Editorial Coordinator: Kimberly O'Brien
Production Manager: Linda Bender
Technical Illustrator: Marcia Cameron
Photographers: Craig Anderson & Dennis Kennedy

ISBN: 1-890621-44-7
This book printed on acid-free paper.
Printed in USA.

10-9-8-7-6-5-4-3-2-1

HOME for the HOLIDAYS

Projects

REJOICE!

Projects

CELEBRATE the SEASON

Projects

SWEET DREAMS

Projects

About the Artist

Happily settled in her Saltbox home studio in Ohio, artist Deb Strain delights in creating bright, cheery folk art tributes to country, gardens, home, and friendship. Her color palette, more intense than traditional folk art, depicts everyday scenes in a wonderfully warm-hearted way.

A former teacher, Deb once painted pattern packages for her friend, doll designer Anne McKinney. Encouraged by the positive response to her work, Deb produced cards that featured her own heartfelt designs, operating her budding business from home. In this epitome of a family-run business, Deb focuses on creating new designs while her husband, Scott, oversees packaging and shipping of orders. Her mother-in-law, Jayne, helps by answering phones and keeping customer service running smoothly and has plenty of welcome assistance from Deb s three eager young children, Arrin, Katie, and Taylor. Deb has experienced great success with prints and fabrics and is thrilled to see her artwork on an ever-increasing number of top-quality licensed products.

Deb's paintings reflect her strong devotion to family and home. She has only to look around her to discover new ideas for artwork. Family vacations, jaunts to antiques stores, and her own pleasant childhood memories provide Deb with an inexhaustible supply of subjects. Possessing a lifelong determination to be an artist, Deb strives to present images that instill joy in all who view them. Her memorable artwork is treasured all around the world by fans who connect emotionally to her charming images and the happiness found in living a simple life.

HOME
for the HOLIDAYS

Projects

* Welcome Home

* Homeward Bound

* Softly Ornamental

* Warm and Fuzzy

* Friends of the Family

* Sweet Accents

* Happy Days

A Warm Welcome

Creating banners, wall hangings, and ornaments as gifts and to decorate your home gets you into the holiday spirit. Everyone who receives your thoughtfully made gifts will be reminded of your friendship throughout the season—and all who enter your home will receive a hearty welcome!

Whether you stage a family fun night to assemble several ornaments or pass a few quiet evenings on your own to embellish a wall hanging, you'll be delighted to display your efforts center stage. Decorating with these artful designs adds color, texture, and style to your home. When the season is over, easily pack the fabric art pieces away to bring out and enjoy next year.

Welcome Home

The perfect place to begin holiday decorating is with a charming panel of fabric printed with lovable snow people. Although it looks finished when you bring it home from the store, batting, backing, machine quilting, and binding bring it to life. Add a rod pocket on the back for handsome hanging.

Then keep going! Add embellishments to make it original. It's so easy to capitalize on the ideas outlined for you. Tack ribbon bows on the packages, use the snowflakes as a printed pattern for embroidered pearl cotton snowflakes, add stars in the sky and beads to the borders. Instructions follow to help you duplicate the wall quilt shown here, but feel free to fly solo on this holiday showpiece.

Materials

- Printed fabric panel (22 x 44")
  We used "Celebrate the Season"
  by Deb Strain for Moda

- 1 yard red print fabric for backing and binding

- Cotton quilt batting (22 x 44")

- 6-inch pieces of 1/4- or 1/8-ribbons
  of your choice (4 used)

- 55 plastic stars (sew-on button style)

- 11 buttons

- 10 small jingle bells

- 84 gold rondelle beads

- 84 gold seed beads

- #3 white pearl cotton

- Rod and finials of choice

- Cord and tassels of choice

How-To

1. Cut backing slightly larger than the printed panel.

2. If desired, make a rod pocket for hanging. Cut a 4 x 22" strip from backing fabric. Hem the short ends. Fold the strip in half lengthwise. Place the raw ends of the strip along the raw ends of the backing, centering it along the width of the back. Stitch in place. Baste the raw edges together and whipstitch the folded edge to the backing fabric, allowing some ease for the rod to fit through.

3. Lay out the backing wrong side up, the batting, then the printed panel, right side up. Pin or baste the layers together. Machine quilt along printed outlines using thread colors of your choice.

4. For quilt binding, cut 2-1/2"-wide strips to total 174" when seamed together. Press strip in half lengthwise. Raw edges together, use a 1/4" seam allowance to stitch binding to all layers, mitering corners and catching rod pocket edges in the seam. Trim layers even. Turn binding to back and stitch the folded edge to the backing.

5. To embellish the panel, embroider snowflakes using straight stitches and French knots in #3 pearl

cotton. On the center top scene of the fabric panel, make French knots using pearl cotton for falling snow.

6. Sew 10 tiny bells to the printed garland on the reindeer. Tie tiny bows from ribbon and tack them on the packages and gate.

7. Center a small seed bead on a larger (rondelle) antique gold bead on each star around the border. Sew in place—the small bead holds the larger one and adds extra dimension.

8. Sew real buttons over the printed buttons on four snow people.

9. Liberally sew plastic button-style stars on the small stars printed on the fabric.

10. If desired, insert rod in pocket on back of panel. Attach finials, and tie on cord and tassels.

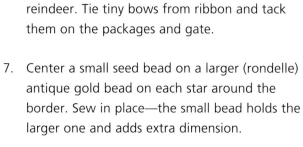

Homeward Bound

As warm as a hug, this charming 19" x 26" wall quilt is bound to be the right size to decorate a special spot in your home. Wherever you say "welcome home"—at the front door, back door, dinner table, or around the fireplace—you'll know where this banner belongs. This wistfully sweet message also makes a lovely gift for your favorite family.

Layer fused fabric pieces as if piecing a puzzle, press in place, and machine appliqué. Personalize with embroidery and beads for a one-of-a-kind masterpiece.

Materials

- 1 yard lightweight fusible webbing
- 1-1/2 yards red print fabric for backing, borders and binding
- 1/2 yard blue fabric for sky
- 1/2 yard white-on-white for snow person
- 1/4 yard white for snow on ground
- Small pieces of 4 different red print fabrics
- Small pieces of 2 blue fabrics for scarf and bird
- Small pieces of 8 different green print fabrics
- Small pieces of 2 different gold or beige print fabrics
- Small piece of black print fabric
- Small piece of orange fabric for carrot nose
- 19 clear plastic paddle wheel beads
- 27 clear plastic beads
- 8 snowflake sequins
- Green, red, black, blue and gold embroidery floss
- 2 small buttons
- Fabric marking pencil
- 20" x 27" piece of cotton batting

How-To

1. Trace the patterns to the paper side of fusible webbing, following manufacturer's directions.

2. Trace the words "Home for the Holidays" onto the snow person fabric, using a fabric marking pencil.

3. Fuse each pattern piece to the fabric selected. Cut out each piece along the pattern lines.

4. From blue for sky, cut a 13-1/2" x 20-1/4" rectangle.

5. Place the snow at the bottom of the blue and fuse in place.

6. Fuse the pieces in this order: snow person body piece, scarf, face, and three hat pieces.

7. Fuse the left and right birdhouses in place, then the center birdhouse. Add the cupola and trim on right birdhouse, then the roofs. Place and fuse the bird, heart, door and base, and the windows. Fuse carrot nose in place.

8. Fuse large birdhouse at the lower left, the main roof piece, the trim and snow pieces, then the blue bird. Fuse small heart at lower right.

9. Machine appliqué using a narrow zig-zag stitch over fabric edges and dimension lines for the snow person arms, hat, and snow, using threads to complement or blend with the fabric.

10. Embellish with embroidery stitches. You may find it easier to slip the needle under just one layer of fabric, rather than through all layers. Stitch "Home for the Holidays" in stem stitch using black floss.

11. Refer to the photograph and illustration to make black French knots for eyes and mouth lines on the snow person and eyes on the birds. Satin stitch using black to make birdhouse windows, and stem stitch birdhouse details.

12. Use green floss for birdhouse details using lazy daisy, stem, and satin stitches. Satin stitch green holly leaves around the heart at lower right.

13. Make French knots using red embroidery floss on birdhouse trim and holly berries. The wing and tail feathers on the red bird are made with French knots and lazy daisy stitches. The heart on the gold birdhouse is satin stitch.

14. With gold floss add details on birdhouses using stem stitch, satin stitch, and French knots. Make gold beaks on the birds.

15. With blue floss, make lazy daisy stitches and French knots for a wing on the blue bird.

16. From red print, cut a 22" × 28" rectangle for backing, 2—3-1/2" × 20-1/4" side border strips and 2—3-1/2" × 19-1/2" top and bottom border strips. Cut 2" binding strips to total 94" when

seamed together end to end. Press the binding in half lengthwise, wrong sides together.

17. Stitch side borders to center panel and press. Sew top and bottom borders to panel and press.

18. Layer the backing, batting, and panel and pin or baste together. Machine quilt 1/4" beyond the edge of the snow person to outline. Machine quilt in-the-ditch along the center panel and borders. Machine quilt a diamond pattern along the borders. Matching raw edges, place binding along borders. Stitch through all layers 1/4" from the edge. Trim backing and batting even with front. Turn binding to the back and stitch the folded edge to the backing.

19. Sew tiny buttons to the center birdhouse roof. Sew clear plastic beads to the sky and snowflake sequins to the snow, securing each with small clear beads.

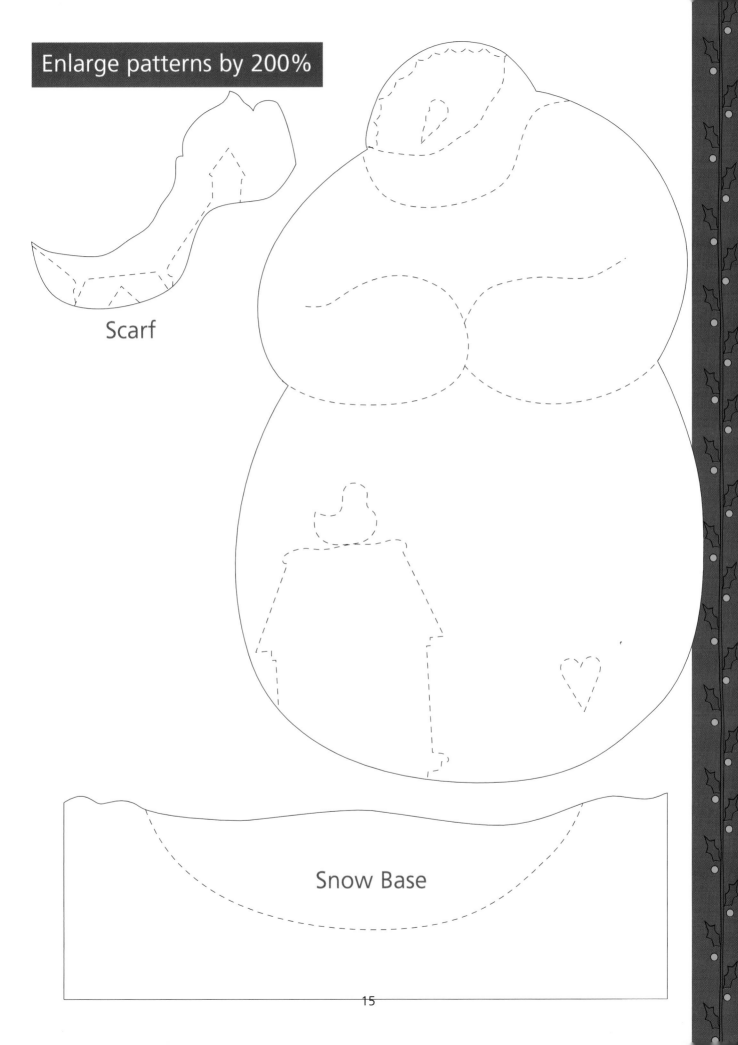

Enlarge patterns by 200%

Scarf

Snow Base

Softly Ornamental

Establish a theme by repeating decorating motifs. These felt ornaments, which are enlarged versions of details from the printed fabric panel, are a great project for the whole family to cut, assemble, and stitch.

Materials

For each tree:

• 3" x 5" piece of gold wool felt

• 3" x 5" piece of green wool felt

• Green and red #3 pearl cotton

• Gold cord for hanging

For each star:

• 5" x 5" piece of red wool felt

• 5" x 5" piece of gold wool felt

• Gold and red #3 pearl cotton

• Gold cord for hanging

How-To

Trees:

1. Using patterns provided, cut large tree from gold felt using pinking shears. Cut small tree from green felt with straight-edge scissors.

2. Center green tree on gold background. Blanket-stitch together with #3 pearl cotton. Make three red French knots and three green lazy daisy stitches on tree. Sew gold hanging cord to the top of the ornament.

Stars:

1. Using patterns provided, cut large star from red felt using pinking shears. Cut small star from gold felt with straight-edge scissors.

2. Center gold star on red background. Blanket-stitch in place with #3 gold pearl cotton. Make three red French knots and five gold lazy daisy stitches on star center. Sew a gold hanging cord to one point.

Warm and Fuzzy

Pearl cotton embroidered snowflakes on wool felt makes snow seem warm and inviting. The motif, borrowed from the fabric panel, creates a look of total coordination.

Tote along this project and embroider a few snowflakes while waiting for your next appointment!

Materials

For each ornament:

- 4" x 4" pieces each of green and red wool felt

- White #3 pearl cotton

- Fabric glue   • Gold cord for hanging

How-To

1. Using patterns provided and pinking shears, cut large circle from green felt and small circle from red felt.

2. Embroider the snowflake design using a double strand of pearl cotton. Make center French knot, straight stitches, then the outer French knots.

3. Center and glue the embroidered red circle to the green wool felt circle.

4. Sew or glue on a gold hanging cord.

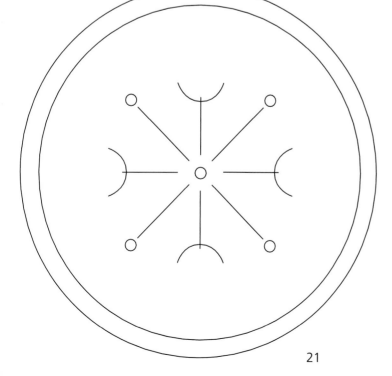

Friends of the Family

Birds of a feather flock together. Welcome your flock with this friendly portrait of a tenderhearted snow person who tends the birdhouses.

This exquisitely detailed appliqué piece is more fun than work to assemble—using fusible webbing and machine stitching to finish it with class. Your creative selection of fabrics make it exclusive. In addition to framing this delightful design, use it on pillows, aprons, jumpers, jackets, sweatshirts, and towels or bedding.

Materials

- 1 yard lightweight fusible webbing
- 1/2 yard dark red background fabric
- 1/2 yard blue for sky
- 1/4 yard white-on-white for snow person
- Small pieces of 5 different red print fabrics
- Small piece of blue print for scarf
- Small pieces of 5 different green print fabrics
- Small pieces of 2 different gold/beige print fabrics
- Small piece of black print fabric
- Small piece of orange for carrot nose
- Green wool felt for holly leaves
- Gold wool felt for two stars
- 26 gold beads
- 6 gold stars
- 26 pearl E beads
- Green, red, and gold embroidery floss
- 5 buttons
- Batting to pad completed project
- 15" x 20" frame

How-To

1. Trace the patterns to paper side of fusible webbing, following manufacturer's directions.

2. Fuse each pattern piece to the fabric selected. Cut out each piece along the outline.

3. From dark red print, cut a 17" × 24" rectangle for the background.

4. Place and fuse the blue sky piece to the rectangle.

5. Fuse the snow person body piece, scarf, face, and three hat pieces in order. Fuse the left and right birdhouses in place; then the center birdhouse. Add the cupola and trim on the right birdhouse, then all roofs. Fuse the bird, bird wing, heart, door and base, and window on center birdhouse. Place and fuse the carrot nose.

6. Machine appliqué using a narrow zig-zag stitch along all fabric edges and to add dimension to the snow person arms and hat, following pattern lines and referring to the photograph.

7. Referring to the photo of the finished project, stitch border lines along the background fabric and embellish the design. Embroider birdhouse details using stem stitch, lazy daisy stitch, and French knots. The bird tail feathers are elongated lazy daisy stitches. Make French knots for snow person eyes and mouth lines. You may find it easier to slip the needle under one layer of fabric rather than through all layers.

8. Sew or glue buttons to the center birdhouse.

9. From green felt, cut 30 holly leaves in three sizes: two smallest leaves for the birdhouse on the left, medium-size leaves on the borders, and the largest leaves at the top of the border. Use a running stitch of green embroidery floss along the center to attach the holly leaves.

10. Stem stitch stems to the holly leaves along the border using gold embroidery floss.

11. Cut two gold felt stars and place on border as shown in photograph. Stitch in place with gold embroidery floss. Sew gold beads and gold stars to the border.

12. Layer batting behind the completed stitchery to add dimension to the design. Frame the piece in a gold frame.

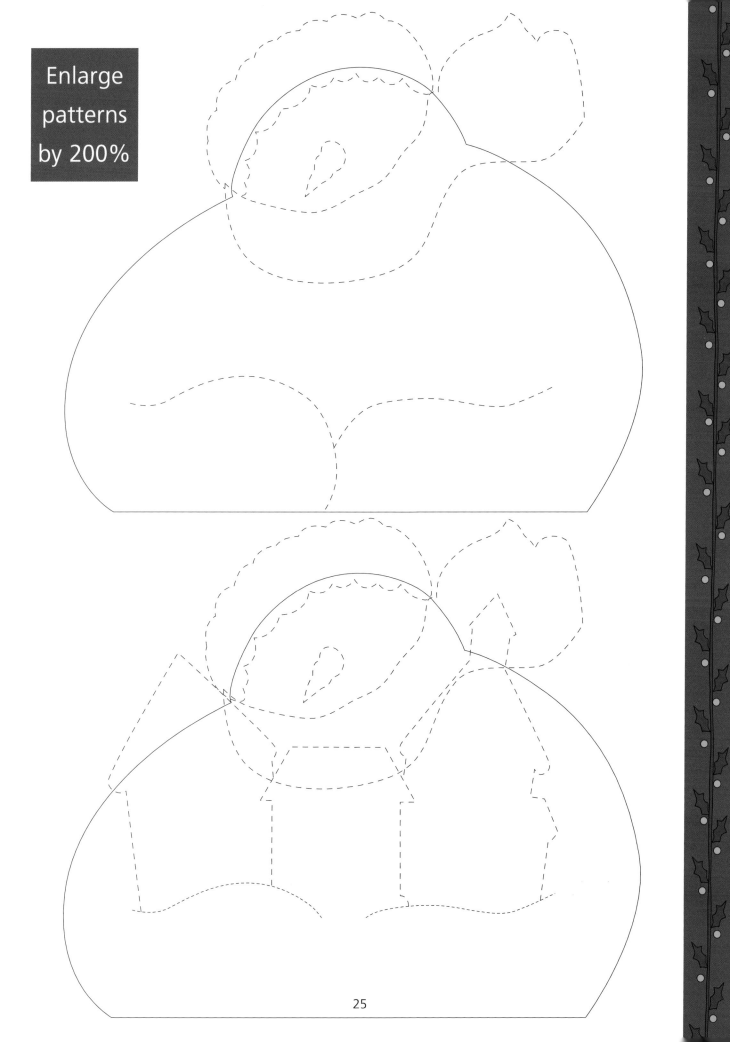

Enlarge
patterns
by 200%

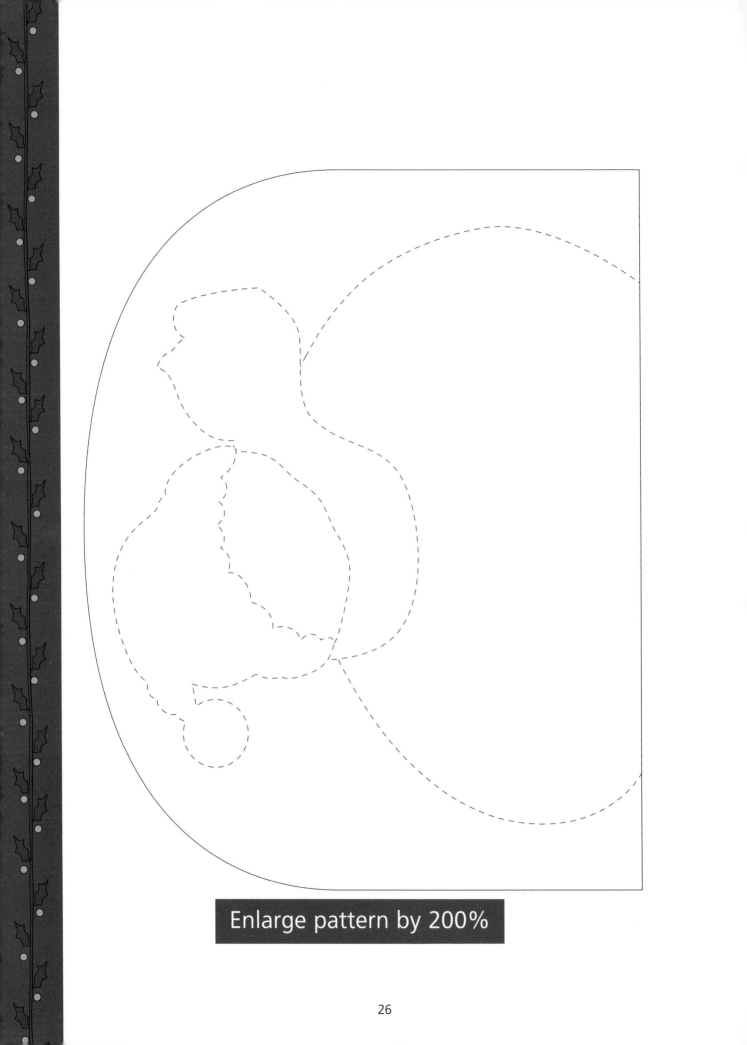

Enlarge pattern by 200%

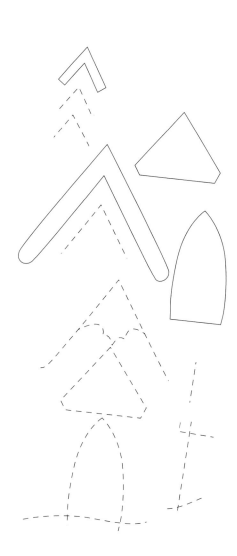
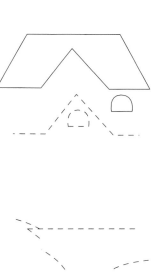

Enlarge patterns by 200%

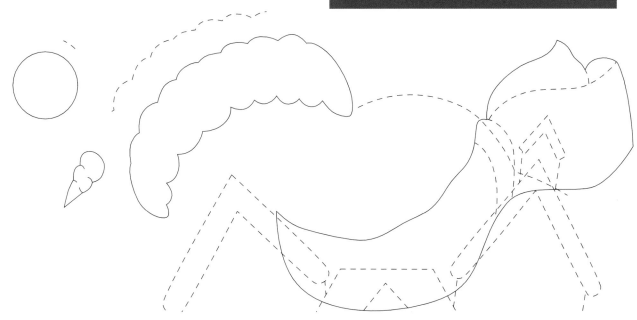

27

Sweet Accents

Longer-lasting than cookies and candy—yet just as sweet—you'll find dozens of uses for these gingerbread men and candy canes. Because neither the felt nor the Ultrasuede require attention to raw edges, the assembly is fast and easy.

Materials

For each candy cane:

- 5" x 8" piece of white felt
- Small pieces of green felt
- 7" x 4" piece of red felt
- 1" x 7" strip of white Ultrasuede

For each gingerbread man:

- 5" x 7" piece of green felt
- 5" x 7" piece of light brown Ultrasuede
- Small pieces of white and red Ultrasuede
- Red and black embroidery floss
- Blush for cheeks

How-To

Candy cane:

1. Using patterns provided, cut candy cane from red felt. Cut one of each leaf from green felt. With pinking shears, cut a 1/2-inch-wide strip from white Ultrasuede.

2. Arrange pieces on white felt. Machine stitch candy cane in place. Stitch a holly leaf to each side; stitch a line along the center of each leaf.

3. Cut and place Ultrasuede strips diagonally on candy cane. Stitch through the center and clip ends flush with candy cane edges.

4. Use pinking shears to trim a narrow white border.

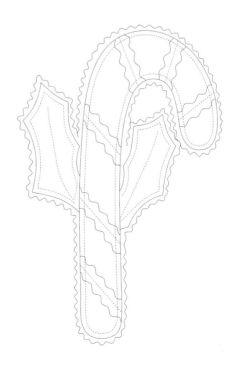

Gingerbread man:

1. Using patterns provided, cut gingerbread man from light brown Ultrasuede; cut heart from red Ultrasuede.

2. Use red floss to stem stitch a mouth. Use black floss to make French knot eyes and straight stitch eyebrows.

3. Place gingerbread man on green felt. Machine stitch close to edges and stitch a line to mark the legs. Stitch heart in place.

4. From white Ultrasuede, cut a 1/2-inch-wide strip. Stitch a piece to each arm, trim ends.

5. With pinking shears, trim green felt, leaving a narrow border around entire ornament.

Happy Days

Celebrate the season. Share the joy expressed by this exuberant snow friend!

Materials

- 1 yard red wool felt
- 1/2 yard green wool felt
- 1/2 yard gold wool felt
- 1-1/4 yards 1/4-inch braid for border
- 1 yard lightweight fusible webbing
- 2/3 yard fabric for background sky
- 1/3 yard white print fabric for snow person
- 1/8 yard gray print fabric
- 1/4 yard print fabric for scarf
- 1/4 yard red fabric for vest and birds
- Small piece green Ultrasuede for vest trim
- Small piece of gold Ultrasuede for trim
- 7" square of Ultrasuede for stick arms
- Small piece orange fabric for nose
- Small piece of fabric for bird nest
- 6 medium size gold star buttons
- 2 large gold star buttons
- 2 gold stars for vest
- 16 small flat gold buttons
- 16 green beads
- 3 black buttons
- 30 clear seed beads
- Black, brown and red embroidery floss; #3 white pearl cotton
- Fabric marking pencil
- 18" × 21" piece of cotton batting
- Blush for cheeks
- Three 1/2" curtain rings
- 36" dowel rod (5/16")

How-To

1. Cut background fabric 18-1/2" × 21-1/2". Use the fabric marking pencil to trace "Celebrate" onto the background fabric.

2. Fuse webbing to the wrong side of gray print fabric. Cut the fabric 4" × 18-1/2", slightly curving the edge. Fuse the piece to the background.

3. Using patterns provided, trace snow person, scarf, nose, birds, and bird nest to paper side of fusible webbing, following manufacturer's directions. Fuse the patterns to fabrics selected and cut out.

4. Fuse snow person body to center of background. Fuse scarf in place. Fuse nose in place.

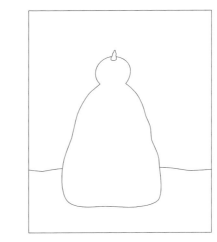

5. Using pattern provided and adding 1 inch on sides and bottom, cut out two vest pieces from red fabric. Use fusible webbing to make a 1-inch hem around the sides and bottom of each vest piece. Cut green Ultrasuede trim, using scalloped edge for vest pattern piece. Using a narrow zig-zag stitch, machine appliqué along front and bottom edges of vest. With black thread, machine feather stitch along two edges of each piece. Stitch green Ultrasuede in place, then machine appliqué around scallops with gold thread.

10. With brown embroidery floss, outline satin stitch letters with stem stitch. With black embroidery floss, make a big smile on the snow person with 8 French knots. Make a black French knot eye on each bird. Make black satin stitches on the cardinal. Straight stitch gold beaks on the birds.

11. Cut a small holly leaf from green felt. Attach it to the bird nest with a straight stitch. Make three red French knot berries.

12. Sew three buttons onto snow person. Make snowflakes on snow person body with white pearl cotton, making 4 straight stitches that overlap at the center. Sew a clear seed bead to the center of each snowflake.

13. Sew a large star button to each twig arm. Use brown embroidery floss to make "hangers" for the stars. Sew 6 gold star buttons randomly around the word "celebrate."

6. Cut out two flowerpot shapes from gold Ultrasuede. Tack in place on each side of the vest with one straight stitch. With black embroidery floss, make a tree shape design with running stitches above each flower pot. Tie floss in a bow on the pot rim. Attach a gold star at top of each tree. Sew a gold button with a green bead to each scallop on the vest trim.

7. Machine appliqué along edges of snow person and nose. Lay vest in place and machine appliqué edge of scarf to hold vest in place. Complete scarf appliqué. Machine appliqué outer vest edges, leaving front and bottom of vest open.

8. Using pattern provided, cut out branches from brown Ultrasuede. Machine stitch in place. Fuse birds and bird nest in place. Machine appliqué birds and nest.

14. From green felt, cut two 3" × 22" strips and two 3" × 18" strips. Along the edges, cut 6 scallops on shorter pieces and 7 scallops on longer pieces.

15. Use the pattern to cut 24 stars from gold felt.

16. Using a zig-zag stitch and matching thread, sew a star to the center of each scallop. Stitch strips to the sides of the appliqué piece.

9. Using machine satin stitch and gold thread, stitch the word "Celebrate."

34

17. From red felt, cut a 24" × 28" rectangle. Place batting behind the appliqué center. Center the piece on the felt, batting between the two pieces. Machine quilt around the appliqué and stitch around the inside of the border.

18. Cut strips of braid; glue them along the seamline between background and green felt border.

19. Scallop the red felt to make a narrow border, using pinking shears. Sew curtain rings to the back of the wall hanging. Insert a dowel through the rings to hang.

Enlarge patterns to 200%

37

Projects

* Show Business

* Snow Guys

* Perfectly Centered

* A Place of Your Own

* Heartfelt

* Spell It Out

REJOICE!

Little Things to Warm Your Heart

For the kid in all of us—especially during the season when memories of holidays past are crystal clear—it's rewarding to create and share handmade projects.

Get creative. Gather family or friends and have fun assembling several of these projects to give to teachers, coworkers, neighbors, and friends—or to make a sales hit at the next crafts bazaar.

The stitchery on the following pages may be small, but they carry lots of weight. When you make them, your special touches give them personality and character. Experience the joy of making holiday decorations again to display and share—whatever your age.

Show Business

This table topper has a story! Used in your home—under a miniature tree or basket of fresh flowers—or made as a gift for the star of this year's performance, you'll be sure to receive a round of applause.

Materials

- 2/3 yard of blue wool felt
- 2/3 yard of white wool felt
- 2/3 yard dark blue background fabric
- 1/4 yard of green, white, and gold print fabrics
- Small pieces of white, green print, gold, brown and red fabrics
- 1/4 yard lightweight fusible webbing
- 6 gold star buttons in 2 sizes
- 8 pearl seed beads
- 21 snowflake sequins
- 21 clear plastic paddle wheel beads
- 21 clear seed beads
- Multicolor miniature Christmas ornaments
- Green pearl cotton
- Black, orange, and brown embroidery floss

How-To

1. From white felt, use pinking shears to cut a 22"-diameter circle. Without cutting through outer edge, cut an 18" circle from the center to make a 2"-wide border.

2. From blue felt, use pinking shears to cut a 23"-diameter circle.

3. From blue print background fabric, cut a 19" circle.

4. Trace patterns for angel, tree, star, the hand-held sign, mittens, wings, heart, and faces onto the paper side of fusible webbing, following manufacturer's instructions. Fuse each pattern to appropriate fabric, then cut out the pieces.

5. Embroider the word "Rejoice" using black floss and a running stitch on white fabric. Use French knots for dots and music notes.

6. Embroider the Christmas play sign using black floss and stem stitch. With brown floss, stitch a free-form tree on the angel using running stitch and French knots.

7. Place the white felt border on the blue background fabric.

8. Fuse the pieces in this order: angel wings, angel, "rejoice" piece, and large star. Next fuse the tree, star on tree, faces on tree and star, mittens and sign on the tree, then the heart on the angel.

9. With matching thread colors, machine appliqué using a narrow zig-zag stitch along fabric edges. Make twig arms on angel and star with machine appliqué stitching. Stitch a post for the Christmas play sign.

10. Embroider faces using French knots, running stitch, and satin stitch.

11. Pin appliquéd piece on blue felt circle. Machine stitch along edges of the white felt border.

12. Sew gold star buttons on background and on the stitched tree on the angel. Sew white seed beads on angel. Make a halo by sewing a loop of gold thread at the top of the angel.

13. Thread miniature Christmas ornaments onto green pearl cotton. Arrange the string of ornaments on tree and tack in place.

14. Top each snowflake sequin with a clear paddle wheel bead, top that with a clear seed bead, and sew on white felt border.

44

Rejoice ♪♩

47

Snow Guys

The more the merrier! These little guys will charm your socks off.
Make them for decorations—make them for gifts.
Make them chubby to stand—make them flat to line up on a garland.
Four patterns are included because the hefty guys require gussets, the thin guys do not.
Size and choice of trims make each snow friend a real character.

Materials

For each Snow Guy:

• 9" square piece of wool felt

• Small strip of felt for scarf

• 2 buttons

• Black and orange embroidery floss

• Polyester fiberfill and polypropylene pellets

• Blush for cheeks

How-To

1. Using patterns provided, cut a front and back for each snowman from felt. Cut a gusset from felt for the flat bottom snowmen.

2. Embroider face using black floss for French knot eyes and orange for satin stitch nose.

3. For the flat bottom version with gusset, use 1/8" seam allowance to sew gusset to front piece, stitching from clip to clip at neck.

4. For both versions, sew the front and back together, leaving a 2" opening on one side to turn. Turn the piece to the right side through the opening. Sew buttons on the front of the snow guy.

5. For the gusseted version, stuff with a thin layer of polyester next to the body; add polypropylene pellets to complete stuffing. Stitch the opening closed. For the non-gusseted version, stuff only with polyester stuffing; stitch the opening closed.

6. From felt cut a 1/2" × 8" rectangle for scarf. Cut a slit in the scarf 2" from one end. Put the scarf around the neck and pull opposite end through the slit. Clip scarf ends for fringe. Blush the cheeks with a bit of color.

49

Perfectly Centered

Holiday or not—this patchwork centerpiece will call attention to any table decoration. Coordinate it with place mats and napkin rings for your dinner table, or change the size to fit other surfaces. This any-time-of-the-year design always adds a homey touch.

Materials

- 2/3 yard backing fabric

- 1/2 yard for center square

- 12 or more fabrics to cut 32 blocks

How-To

1. Cut an 18-1/2" square of backing fabric.

2. Cut a 14-1/2" center square. Cut 32 total 2-1/2" squares from fabrics.

3. Use 1/4-inch seams throughout project. Alternating fabrics, join two rows of 7 blocks each and two rows of 9 blocks each. Press seams.

4. Sew 7-block strips to opposite sides of the center square. Sew 9-block strips to top and bottom of square. Press.

5. Right sides together, place pieced top on backing piece. Stitch around piece, leaving a 4" opening for turning. Turn to right side; stitch opening closed.

A Place of Your Own

Welcome to the table! The warm and friendly message is clear, delivered
by your colorful, handmade place mats. Perfectly coordinated, yet
delightfully different, these quilt-style linens will enhance your holiday pottery.

Materials

- 14" × 18" piece of wool felt
- 1/3 yard of background fabric
- 1/4 yard border fabric
- Small pieces of 12 different fabrics for blocks
- Small piece of red print fabric for hearts
- 12" × 16" piece of batting
- 1/3 yard fusible webbing

How-To

1. Cut a 9-1/2" × 13-1/2" rectangle from background fabric.

2. Fuse webbing to fabric pieces for quilt blocks. From the fabric, cut 2-1/2" squares.

3. Arrange the fabric blocks on the background fabric, spacing approximately 3/8" vertically and 5/8" horizontally apart. Fuse the blocks in place.

4. From fabric for the border, cut two 2"-wide strips. From one strip, cut two 2" squares.

5. Using pattern provided, trace heart four times to fusible webbing backing. Fuse hearts to red fabric and cut out; fuse hearts to the 2" squares.

6. Cut two 9-1/2" lengths from the strips (Step 4) and sew one to each side of the appliquéd background, using 1/4-inch seam allowance. Press seams toward the border. Cut two 13-1/2" strips. Sew each 2" square with a heart to opposite ends of the strips. Sew a length to the top and a length to the bottom of the place mat. Press.

7. Machine appliqué blocks and hearts using a narrow zig-zag along fabric edges.

8. Place batting on wrong side of place mat; trim 1/2" smaller all around than the fabric.

9. Use pinking shears to cut gold felt 13-1/2" × 17-1/2". Center place mat and batting on the felt. Machine quilt in-the-ditch between the background fabric and border. Machine appliqué outer edge of border to felt.

Heartfelt

When you love having friends and family at your dinner table,
put your whole heart into it. Felt, cotton print fabric, a simple button,
and grosgrain ribbon work well together in this cheery napkin ring.
Coordinate it with a patchwork centerpiece and place mats for classic country style.

Materials

- 4" square of fusible webbing
- 4" square of wool felt
- 4" square of cotton fabric
- 7/8" button
- 20-inch piece of 5/8" grosgrain ribbon

How-To

1. Using patterns provided, cut large heart from wool felt using pinking shears.

2. Trace small heart to backing of fusible webbing. Fuse webbing to cotton fabric. Cut out heart and remove backing.

3. Machine appliqué using a narrow zig-zag stitch over raw edge of heart using matching thread.

4. Place button in center of heart. Place a 20" length of grosgrain ribbon on the back. Sew on button, sewing through the center of the ribbon on the back.

Spell it Out

Sweet snow people spell L O V E lined up any way you please.
Each charming character has personality. Add your creativity and
change the letters to spell out a name or other personal expression.

Materials

- 1 yard lightweight fusible webbing

- Four 6-1/4" × 10-1/4" soft green wool felt pieces

- 1/4 yard winter-white wool felt

- Small pieces of black, red and gold wool felt

- 1/4 yard blue print background fabric

- Small piece of white print "snow" fabric

- Small pieces of 4 red fabrics

- Small pieces of 3 green fabrics

- Small pieces of 3 blue fabrics

- Small piece of beige fabric

- Gold and black embroidery floss

- 4 flower appliqués

- 1 button

How-To

1. With pinking shears, cut four 6-1/4" × 10-1/4" rectangles from soft green felt.

2. Fuse webbing to back of blue background fabric. From background fabric, cut four 5-3/4 × 10-1/4" pieces. Fuse webbing to back of white snow fabric and cut four 1-3/4" × 5-3/4" pieces. Remove backing and fuse white to each blue piece. Trim the four pieces to 5-1/4" × 9-3/4" with pinking shears. Center on green felt and fuse in place.

3. Using patterns provided, trace each piece to the paper backing of fusible webbing.

4. Fuse snow people to winter-white wool felt. Fuse other pattern pieces to fabric selected. Cut out.

5. Fuse snow person body, scarf, and head to background pieces. Add aprons, squares, letters, then the felt hats.

6. Matching threads to fabrics, machine appliqué using a narrow zig-zag stitch around all raw edges, and stitch details. **Note:** We did not stitch around the letters.

7. Use black embroidery floss to embroider eyes and mouths, and French knots and straight stitches for the features. With gold embroidery floss and a satin stitch, make carrot noses.

8. Cut a heart from red wool felt, and tack it in place with black floss tied in a bow. Tack flower appliqués to the heads and hats.

61

63

CELEBRATE the SEASON

Projects

* All Wrapped Up

* Wear Your Mittens

* Treats for the Cook

* Tote a Merry Wish

* Look for the Lining

Gifts for Everyone

Look here for last-minute gifts that you can make in an afternoon or evening.

Purchase such basics as papier-mâché boxes, aprons, towels, mitts, and baskets. Use your favorite holiday designs from the printed fabric panel to embellish the basics and coordinate as many gifts as you have time to make.

Projects, such as the handy tote bag and basket liner, encourage you to make whatever size suits you or the gift recipient. As you stitch these projects, you're sure to be inspired to make even more gifts to celebrate the season.

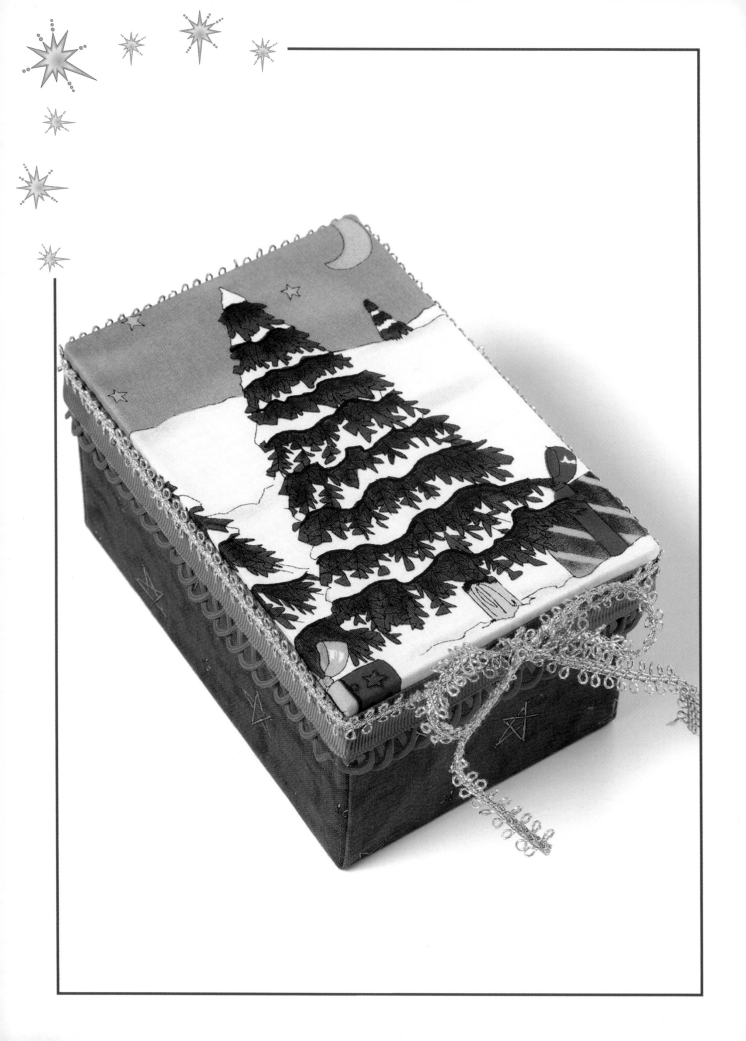

All Wrapped Up

Which is the gift—what's inside or the beautifully trimmed box? Make this treasure, which serves dual purposes, from myriad shapes and sizes of boxes. Cover the containers with your favorite holiday scenes and embellishments.

Materials

- Purchased box
- Printed design from fabric panel to fit box
- Fabric to cover box or paint for box
- Trimming materials as desired
- Fabric glue

How-To

1. Paint or cover the box bottom with fabric, using a light coat of glue. Let the paint or glue dry.

2. Cut out holiday design for box lid and glue in place. Embellish with ribbon, braid, artificial leaves and berries, or other trims.

Wear Your Mittens

One of our favorite things, warm woolen mittens are best when made for a friend. Lined with flannel, these quick-to-stitch chill-chasers are bound to please. A matching scarf, decorated with a holiday design, completes the gift perfectly. Make the set easily in an afternoon.

Materials

- 1/2 yard wool
- Snow Friends printed panel
- 1/4 yard lightweight fusible webbing
- 1/4 yard cotton flannel
- Small strip cotton print
- 1/2 yard 1/4" elastic
- 16 small jingle bells
- 6 gold star buttons

How-To

1. Cut a 9" strip of 54-inch wool for the scarf. Cut a design from printed panel (design used is 6" × 8"). Fuse webbing to back of design, cut out on design borders. Place design 5" from scarf end and fuse together. Machine appliqué design to scarf.

2. Machine stitch a 1/4" hem on long scarf edges; stitch 1-1/2" hems on the ends. Evenly space 5 gold star buttons below the design. Sew a gold star to the printed design.

3. Using patterns and wool, cut 2 of each of the 4 mitten pieces, reversing one set to make a right and left mitten. From cotton flannel, cut 2 of each of the 4 mitten pieces.

4. Place flannel piece on each wool piece. Right sides together (flannel side is wrong side), use a scant 1/4" seam to stitch thumb gusset to palm side. Stitch thumb to gusset/palm. Stitch outer edge of mitten back to palm. Sew a 2" band of contrasting fabric to wrist; turn half to inside and topstitch to make a cuff. Stitch a 1/2" casing for elastic 2" below the cuff edge. Insert elastic.

5. Sew bells between the band on the cuff and the elastic casing.

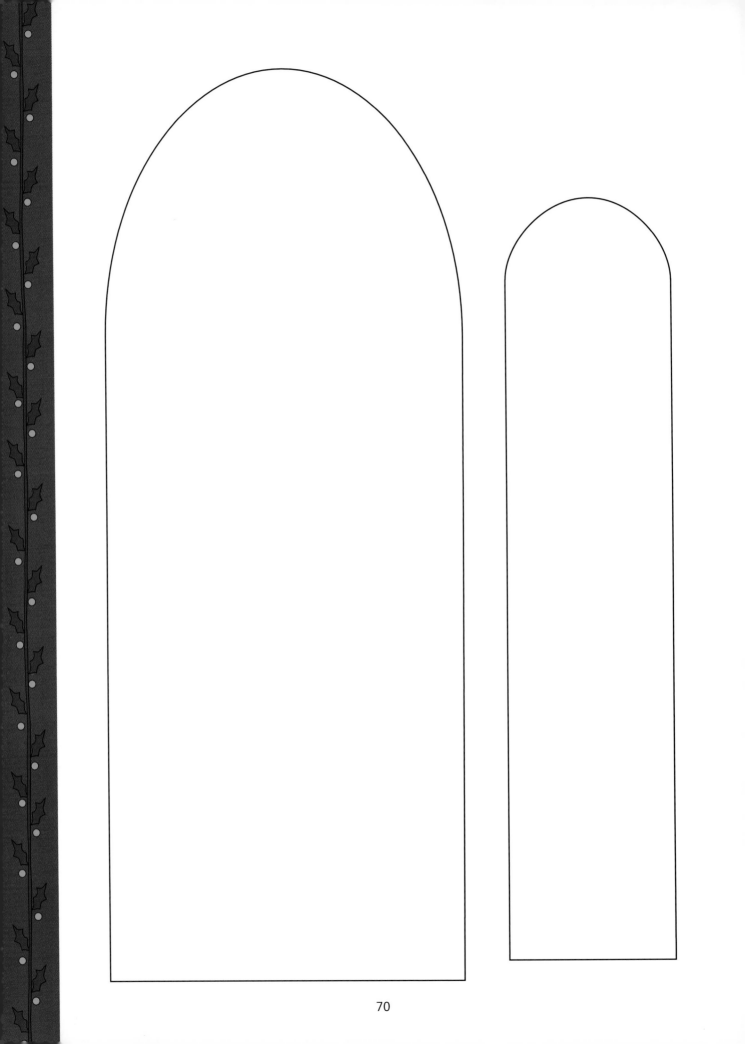

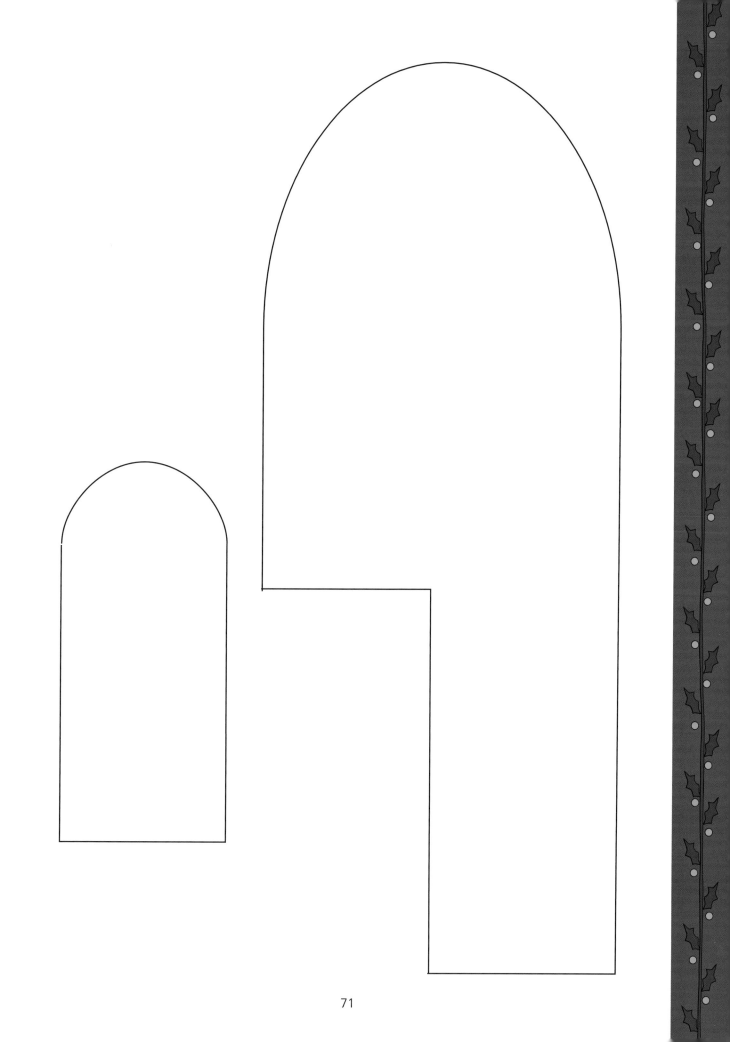

Treats for the Cook

With or without edible accompaniments, these kitchen gifts will please any palate.
embellish a purchased apron, kitchen towels, and oven mitt with delightful designs
from the printed fabric panels. These gifts have that made-to-order,
fully coordinated look that discerning chefs will appreciate.

Materials

- Purchased apron with pocket front
- Two purchased towels
- Quilted oven mitt
- Small piece fusible webbing
- printed fabric panel
- Strips of three cotton prints
- 1/2 yard jumbo rick-rack
- 1 yard regular rick-rack

How-To

Apron

1. Cut printed panel 1" larger than apron pocket. Stitch rick-rack 1/2" from right side of fabric edge and stitch along the center. Turn fabric to back, allowing trim to edge the panel. Topstitch close to the folded edge. Turn under remaining sides 1/2" and press. Place panel on pocket. Stitch in place, stitching through pocket divider.

2. Fuse webbing to 2" × 8" border piece; cut along border lines. Fuse border to apron bib. Machine appliqué over fabric edges.

Oven Mitt

1. From print fabric, cut a 5"-wide piece to fit the wrist opening plus seam allowance. Stitch short ends together to make a loop. Press loop in half lengthwise. Sew raw edge of cuff to inside of mitt along the opening. Fold cuff to right side of mitt.

2. For a hanging loop, cut a 1-1/2" × 6" strip. Fold strip in half and turn raw edge to meet fold. Stitch along the edges. Raw ends together, sew the loop to the inside of the mitt. Sew bells or trim to cuff.

Towels

1. Cut a border strip and trim, if desired, to fit towel width. Stitch trim to right side of fabric edge, turn trim to back and press. Fuse and topstitch trimmed band to towel, or machine appliqué the untrimmed band to the towel.

Tote a Merry Wish

Carry an armload of gifts or necessities in a bag made to size. Frame a "Celebrate" design with ribbon, sew a few seams, attach carrying handles, and line it with wool felt for strength and durability.

Materials

- 1 yard wool felt
- printed fabric panel
- 1/3 yard fusible webbing
- 1-1/4 yards cotton print fabric
- 1-1/2 yards 5/8"-wide grosgrain ribbon to frame printed design
- 1-1/2 yards 5/8"-wide grosgrain ribbon for handles
- 1" buttons to trim bag

How-To

1. From cotton print, cut two 14" × 16" rectangles for the bag front and back. Cut a 7" × 44" strip for continuous sides and bottom panel, piecing the length if necessary.

2. Fuse webbing to back of printed fabric panel. Cut out the panel and fuse rectangle for bag front. Topstitch grosgrain ribbon along the fabric panel edges, mitering the ribbon along the corners.

3. From wool felt cut two 14" × 18" lining pieces for front and back, one 7" × 44" strip for continuous side and bottom lining (piecing if necessary), and two 22" strips for handles. Sew grosgrain ribbon to the handles, trim the handles with pinking sheers.

4. Sew opposite long edges of the sides/bottom strip to the front and back pieces. Sew lining together in the same manner.

5. Fit the lining inside the bag, wrong sides together. Turn the top of the lining to the outside of the bag to create a cuff. Trim the cuff with pinking sheers.

6. Position and sew the handles to the bag, securing them with buttons along the felt cuff. Sew additional buttons along the cuff.

Look for the Lining

A basket with a fabric liner is as good as the silver that follows the clouds.
For gift-giving, liners are the refined extra in baskets loaded with goodies.
Adapt the instructions for this quick-to-make liner to any basket size.

Materials

- Basket of your choice

- 3/4 yard fabric (larger baskets require more, or combine complementary fabrics)

How-To

1. Trace around the bottom of the basket; add 1" all around, and cut out the shape for the liner bottom.

2. For the liner sides, measure the basket height and the circumference of the top of the basket. Add 1" to both measurements. (For example, a basket 8" high and 30" around the top equals 9" × 31".) Note the measurement. Cut a fabric strip to this size.

3. Stitch a gathering line along one long edge of the strip. Right sides together, match raw edges, and evenly fit the gathered edge to the liner bottom, pinning it in place. Sew together with a scant 1/2" seam.

4. For the ruffle, cut a 5"-wide strip 1-1/2 times the circumference of the liner, piecing the strip for length if necessary. (If the basket has a handle, cut the length of the strip in half and make two separate ruffles to fit around the handle.) Fold the strip in half lengthwise, wrong sides together, and press. (For two strips, fold right sides together, stitch the short ends, turn to right side, and press.) Stitch a gathering line along the raw edges of the ruffle.

5. Right sides together, gather, pin, and sew the ruffle to the top edge of the liner, using a scant 1/2" seam allowance. Place the liner in the basket.

SWEET DREAMS

All Through the House

Extend your gifts and home decorating creativity past the holidays. You'll want to keep these projects present to warm you and your home during chilly winter months and well into spring.

From the charming door trim that could be used to signal nap-time for baby to the adorable pillows that invite imaginative story-telling and the bed quilt that can be made any size you wish, you'll be planning not only this season's projects, but also some for next season.

Coordinate a whole room of accessories. Or create individual projects to suit just the right person.

Projects

* Cat Nap

* On Top of the World

* Star Bright Quilt

Cat Nap

Encourage "Peace on Earth" with this starry night version of a napping snowman and his cat. This charming appliqué would be adorable on a large background for an inviting pillow, or applied to a cat-lover's jacket or shirt.

Materials

- 1/4 yard lightweight fusible webbing

- 1/3 yard moons and stars fabric for background

- 8"-square of gold fabric for moon

- Small pieces of white, red, green, and gold fabrics for snowman, scarf, nightcap, and star

- Small pieces of beige and white Ultrasuede for cat

- 33 gold seed beads

- 5 larger gold beads

- 1 gold star bead

- 1 yard gold-and-white stripe cording

- 2-1/2 yards 5/8" yellow satin ribbon

- 26" length of 1/4" elastic

- 8" cardboard circle

- 10" circle of muslin for backing

- Fabric glue

- 8" circle of white felt

- 8" circle of cotton batting

- Black and gold embroidery floss

- #3 white pearl cotton

How-To

1. From background fabric cut a 10" circle.

2. Trace moon, star, snowman, scarf, cap, and cat patterns to fusible webbing. Fuse to appropriate fabrics for each piece. Cut out pieces. Remove paper backing as you fuse pieces to background fabric.

3. Fuse moon to background, then snowman body, scarf, hat, star, and cat.

4. Machine appliqué along fabric edges and to define design as shown on pattern pieces and photograph.

5. Machine stitch cat details as shown on pattern. Embroider additional details. With gold floss make nose using satin stitches outlined with stem stitch.

Make snowman eyelids with two straight stitches and black floss. Embroider cat whiskers and mouth with straight stitches; make black French knots for eyes and nose. With white pearl cotton, make French knots on cat ears. Use straight stitches with pearl cotton to make a hanger to connect the star and the moon.

6. Sew gold seed beads on the moon. Sew larger gold beads to star points. Sew a gold star bead to the tip of the snowman's nightcap.

7. From muslin, cut a 10" circle. Layer muslin, cotton batting, and the appliqué piece; pin the layers together. Use contasting thread to machine quilt 1/4" beyond the appliqué shape.

8. Center the appliqué piece on a cardboard circle, and pull fabric evenly to the back. Glue the fabric edges to the back of the cardboard.

9. Cut a 48" length of satin ribbon. Stitch a gathering line close to one edge. Gather threads to fit cardboard diameter. Stitch stripe cording to cover gathering line. Stitch cord and ribbon to the length of elastic.

10. Wrap and glue the ribbon edging around the fabric-covered cardboard edge. Overlap ends and secure to back of cardboard.

11. Fold remaining ribbon in half. Tack the fold to the back of the piece for hanging. Glue a white felt circle to the back to finish.

On Top of the World

Snow people decked in finery perch confidently upon the moon.
Plump these pillows on a bed to incite plenty of giggles and pleas for stories of the
moon, stars, and snow friends. These soft accents will be perfectly at home all winter.

Materials

For each pillow:

- 3/4 yard fabric for back, border, and binding

- 1/2 yard muslin for backing

- 1/2 yard fusible webbing

- 1/2 yard fabric for sky background

- 1/3 yard fabric for moon

- Small pieces of white print for snow person

- Small piece of gold print fabric for star

- Black, green, and gold embroidery floss

- #3 white pearl cotton

- Blush for cheeks

- 2 yards cotton cording

- Two 16"-squares of cotton batting

- 16" square pillow form

Additional materials for Ski Buff Pillow

- Red fabric for sweater and hat

- 2 green print fabrics

- 1 small jingle bell

Additional materials for Snow Lady Pillow

- Red print fabric for jacket

- 2 green print fabrics for dress and scarf

- White fabric for birdhouse

- 2 gold star buttons

- Silk ribbon for ribbon roses
or purchased flower appliques

Additional materials for Marching Snowman Pillow

- 2 red print fabrics for vest and hat trim

- Green print for scarf

- Green Ultrasuede for vest trim

- 10 gold beads

How-To

1. From red fabric, cut one 16-1/2" square for pillow back, two 2" × 16-1/2" border strips, and two 2" × 13-1/2" border strips. Cut 1"-wide bias strips to total 66 inches when seamed together.

2. From muslin cut two 16-1/2" squares for backing.

3. From background for sky, cut one 13-1/2" square.

Ski Buff Pillow:

1. Using patterns provided, trace moon, star, legs, hands, face, hat, sweater, sweater band, sweater cuffs, scarf, and hat band to fusible webbing. Fuse webbing to fabrics for each piece and cut out each piece.

2. Remove paper backing as you fuse each piece. Fuse moon and star to background sky fabric. Fuse sweater, legs, and hands, scarf, face, and hat, then hat band, sweater band, and sweater cuffs.

3. Machine appliqué using coordinating threads over fabric edges and to define lines.

4. Embroider details. Use gold satin stitches outlined with stem stitch for nose and sweater border. Make black French knot eyes. Add two straight stitches to attach star to moon. With white pearl cotton add French knots to hat band and sweater cuffs. Make snowflakes on sweater border with straight stitches.

5. Tack a jingle bell to the tip of the hat. Add a touch of blush to the cheeks.

6. Using 1/4" seams, stitch a 13-1/2" border strip to each side. Stitch a 16-1/2" border strip to top and

bottom. Layer muslin, cotton batting, and pillow front. Machine quilt 1/4" beyond the appliquéd design. Machine quilt in-the-ditch between the border and background fabric.

7. Insert cording in bias strips, or purchase cording, and sew to pillow front.

8. Place pillow backing and front right sides together. Stitch together, leaving an 8" opening to turn. Turn cover to right side, insert pillow form, and whipstitch opening closed.

Snow Lady Pillow:

1. Trace patterns for moon, star, legs, hands, face, jacket, dress, scarf, and birdhouse to fusible webbing. Fuse webbing to appropriate fabrics for each piece; cut out each piece.

2. Remove paper backing as you fuse each piece. Fuse moon and star, legs, dress, jacket, scarf, face and hands, and birdhouse in place.

3. Machine appliqué using coordinating threads over fabric edges; to make the pole, roof, and birdhouse base; and to define lines.

4. Embroider details. Use gold to satin stitch a nose and outline with stem stitch. Use black for eyes and heart-shape birdhouse door. Make two

straight stitches to attach star to moon. Make eyes with French knots, and straight stitch brows. Satin stitch the heart on the birdhouse. Use green

floss with stem and lazy daisy stitches for a vine on the birdhouse pole. Make a white pearl cotton French knot perch for the birdhouse.

5. Embroider silk ribbon flowers and leaves on birdhouse pole and on snow lady's head, or tack on purchased flower appliqués. Stitch two button stars on jacket. Add blush to her cheek!

6. Using 1/4" seams, stitch a 13-1/2" border strip to each side. Stitch a 16-1/2" border strip to top and bottom. Layer muslin, batting, and pillow front. Machine quilt 1/4" beyond the appliquéd design. Machine quilt in-the-ditch between the border and background fabric.

7. Insert cording in bias strips, or use purchased cording, and stitch to the pillow top edge, matching raw edges.

8. Place backing and front right sides together and stitch together, leaving an 8" opening to turn.

Turn cover to right side, insert pillow form, and whipstitch opening closed.

Marching Snowman Pillow:

1. Trace moon, star, snowman body, vest, vest border, scarf, hat, and hat band to fusible webbing. Fuse webbing to fabrics for each piece; cut out each piece.

2. Remove paper backing as you fuse each piece. Fuse moon, snowman body, vest, scarf, vest border, hat, hat band, and star in place.

3. Machine appliqué using coordinating threads over fabric edges and to define lines.

4. Embroider details. Use gold to satin stitch nose, outline with stem stitch. Make mouth and eyes with black French knots. Add black straight stitches for eye brows. Sew 10 gold beads to vest trim. Add a touch of blush to his cheek!

5. Using 1/4" seams, stitch a 13-1/2" border strip to each side. Stitch a 16-1/2" border strip to top and bottom. Layer muslin, batting, and pillow front.

Machine quilt 1/4" beyond the appliquéd design. Machine quilt in-the-ditch between the border and background fabric.

6. Insert cording in bias strips, or purchase cording, and stitch to pillow front, matching raw edges.

7. Right sides together, stitch backing to pillow front, leaving an 8" opening to turn. Turn cover to right side, insert pillow form, and whipstitch opening closed.

Ski Buff Pillow

Snow Lady Pillow

Ski Buff Pillow

91

Marching Snowman Pillow

Marching Snowman Pillow

Star Bright Quilt

Wrap up to dream of starry nights. This brilliant year-round addition to your home is made with basic Nine-Patch blocks and easier-than-they-look star points. Instructions are for a 60" x 72" quilt—it's just as delightful larger or smaller.

Materials

- 4 yards backing fabric

- 1-3/4 yards dark blue stripe for blocks

- 1-1/2 yards light blue print for blocks

- 1-1/2 yards blue with gold star print

- 2 yards gold print for star points, centers, and binding

- 66" x 78" cotton batting

- Pearl cotton to tie quilt

How-To

1. From dark blue stripe, cut 150—3-1/2" squares. From light blue print, cut 120—3-1/2" squares.

2. From gold, cut 42—3" squares. Using Pattern A, cut 142 points; reverse the pattern and cut 142 points.

3. Also from gold fabric, cut 7—2-1/2"-wide strips. Sew the strips together end to end to make a continuous length to use for the binding.

4. From blue with gold star print, cut 71 of Pattern B.

5. Sew together 3 rows of 3-1/2" dark blue and light blue squares, referring to the illustration for placement. Press seams toward dark blue squares. Sew together the rows to make a 9-1/2" square, including seam allowance. Make 30 Nine-Patch blocks.

6. Sew four Pattern A points to each Pattern B piece, noting placement. Press seams toward the gold fabric. Repeat to make 71 units.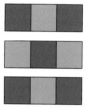

7. Lay out 6 rows of Nine-Patch blocks with point units alongside the blocks. Sew the rows together.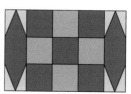

9. Lay out 7 rows using the remaining point units and the 3" gold squares, placing squares between each unit and at the end of the units.

10. Lay out the rows of point units with gold squares and the rows of Nine-Patch blocks with point units, beginning and ending with a row of point units with gold squares. Sew the rows together, butting seams for a neat finish. Press the seams in one direction.

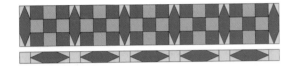

11. Cut and piece backing fabric to measure at least 3" larger all around than the quilt top. Press the seams in one direction.

12. Lay out the backing on a smooth surface, wrong side up, and secure it in place. Fluff and layer the batting. Place the quilt top right side up on the layers; pin or baste through all layers.

13. Use pearl cotton to tie at the corners of the gold star squares.

14. Fold the binding in half lengthwise and press. Raw edges together, sew the binding to the quilt top using a 1/4" seam, mitering the corners and overlaping the binding ends. Turn the binding to the backing and hand stitch the folded edge to the backing.

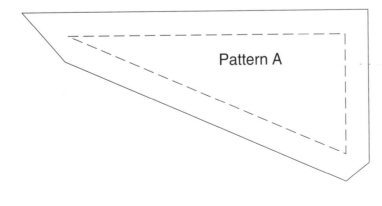

Pattern A

Pattern B